FAST
FROM WRONG
THINKING

GREGORY DICKOW

Fast from Wrong Thinking

A 40-Day Journey to Change from The Inside Out

For information, please write

Gregory Dickow Ministries
PO Box 7000
Chicago, IL 60680

or visit us online at:

www.gregorydickow.com

GREGORY**DICKOW**

@gregorydickow

gregorydickow.com

Table of Contents

What Others Are Saying

"The testimony of Jesus is the spirit of prophecy."
Revelation 19:10.

We constantly receive miraculous testimonies from people who have experienced firsthand the power of fasting from wrong thinking. Here are just a few of them. Let their stories serve as a prophecy, or prediction, of the great things that you can expect to happen in your life. Get ready for *your* revolution—from the inside out!
—Gregory Dickow

50-year addiction broken

I recently completed your 40-day Fast From Wrong Thinking. As a result, I quit smoking shortly after! I had smoked for over 50 years of my life, now I've been four months clean, with no craving at all! Only God! Thank you, Pastor Dickow, for being real, and doing all that God has planned for you, according to His will. Amen! **—Debrah**

No longer suicidal

Thank you very much for the emails and messages on the Fast From Wrong Thinking! They helped me so much! I was even able to share them with a former colleague, who had just received negative medical news and was threatening to commit suicide! But this message of HOPE made all the difference! **—Mary**

Marriage restored

I began to receive the 40-day Fast From Wrong Thinking during a very bad time in my marriage. My wife moved out, and I realized she wasn't coming back. About 20 days into the Fast From Wrong Thinking, I angrily told her to get out of the house. Four days passed, and I realized that she wasn't coming back. She said the pain she felt was too much. On day 38 of the Fast From Wrong Thinking, it still looked hopeless.

But on day 39, I read your message and began to expect the tables to turn. At noon, my wife came home! Something had happened in her heart, and she felt she could give me this one last chance for our family. The Lord restored my family back, and I know I'm a different man now! —**James**

Son changed in prison

My 19-year-old son had been incarcerated; and while in prison, I had been sending him copies of the Fast From Wrong Thinking. As a result, he rededicated his life to the Lord, and he began ministering to others and leading them to Christ—right in the prison! He and the other inmates love the Fast From Wrong Thinking. Within two weeks, he was released from prison, and the charges were miraculously dropped! —**Christine**

Free from anxiety

Since I have been doing the Fast From Wrong Thinking, I feel like I have been to a therapist! I find I am not feeling anxious or weighed down with situations! As soon as a bad thought comes, I just cast it out—it is the most freeing thing I have done! Thank you so much, Gregory Dickow!
—**Joan**

Freed from anger

Dear Pastor, I have noticed a wonderful change in my everyday life. My thinking is changing, and my actions are following. I have noticed how I handled a situation with my husband. Anger did not control me. Neither did emotional bashing of myself. I am accepting that I have rights because Jesus gave me these rights. There have been times when the old thinking tries to come into play, but I find myself trying to remember what thought should I replace it with. The thought on Day 27 was especially meaningful to me, and when I read it for the first time, it touched me deep inside. I felt like I wanted to cry. I have confidence now over that negative thought that has plagued me my whole adult life. Thank you! —**Marie**

Healed of PTSD

I praise God that you were obedient to God to start the Fast From Wrong Thinking. I don't want to know, nor will I think of where my life would be without going through it.

I never stopped this life-changing fast and was healed of a lifetime of post-traumatic stress disorder! If you've never had it, you don't want to know what that's like. I praise God daily for my healing. Thank you again! —**Vicky**

Healed from Kidney failure

When I began FFWT, I thought I was a pretty positive person. While on the journey, I began to realize that I had some major issues buried. So much from my past had been hidden for so long and was causing havoc on my health. However, when I continued the journey with FFWT, everyday and every email would be just what I needed! Yesterday, I had a checkup with my renal (REE-NAL) doctor. I was at major risk for kidney failure but stood on the promises of God shared through the FFWT. My doctor told me that my kidney levels had improved, my blood pressure was lower than it had been in over 2 years (108/78), my weight was down, and he said don't come back until March 2019, to monitor them! Thank you, Pastor, for being obedient and sharing FFWT with us! —**Belinda**

Survivor of disastrous events

After suffering the disastrous effects of Hurricanes Irma and especially Maria in Puerto Rico, I went completely blank on purpose, ambition, motivation or anything that resembled God's grace. The Lord brought me to Pastor Dickow, whom I watched before, but lost my way. The

Lord brought the 40 Day Fast into my life and my reintroduction to being without limits, no matter what, because He's a big, big, God. Thank you Pastor Dickow for "renewing my mind" back to the spiritual power which was given to me on the cross. God bless you and all of you who love the Lord and follow "Dickow." —**Marie**

Freed from fear

Over 10 years ago, my ex-boyfriend tried to kill me. He sliced my throat, stabbed me multiple times, and left me in a ditch for dead. For years I have lived in fear of what he would do if he finds me when released from prison. Six days into the Fast From Wrong Thinking, the feeling of fear has left me completely! I know now, more than ever, that I serve a God bigger than any abuse I have ever faced. I look forward to the testimonies to come over the next 40 days! —**Charlotte**

Free from 31-year addiction

Pastor Dickow, I have gotten so much from your Fasting From Wrong Thinking. I am learning to apply *His Word* to my everyday life. I have never felt so free in my entire life. I am now free from a 31-year addiction, and it's only the grace of God that I'm alive to share this with you. Before this year, I knew Jesus, but not personally. Now I know God is faithful, and I am going to succeed in making something good out of all the bad. —**Betsy**

Lost 11 pounds

I started the Fast From Wrong Thinking and I lost 11 pounds without even trying! I didn't even have the desire for eating as much when I started changing the way I thought. During that time, I went to my doctor for a checkup and he was so surprised, he asked me, "What diet are you on?" I looked at him and said, "Diet nothing! I went on a Fast From Wrong Thinking with Gregory Dickow! —**Amber**

Healed from Insomnia

You need to know that during the last 40-day Fast From Wrong Thinking, I was completely healed from insomnia after many years. I can finally sleep through the night. I wake up refreshed and renewed! Fasting from wrong thinking has changed everything. —**Samuel**

Patients healed

I am a Christian counselor. Our ministry works with marriages and individuals in crisis, and your Fast From Wrong Thinking has been a great tool that God has used to help bring His truth and His healing to our clients. It is amazing how often our clients would need the exact word God had given you for that day. God has ministered greatly to me as an individual believer, as well as my clients, through this fast. Thank you for being willing to be such an effective conduit for God's truth and power to flow through. —**Jerry**

Introduction
Changed: From the Inside Out

We are about to go on an unprecedented journey, which carries with it the remarkable DNA of change!

A number of years ago, I was frustrated when I saw so many people desiring change in their lives, but failing to see results. Out of this frustration, I believe God spoke to me and said, "Call My people to **fast from wrong thinking**." In that moment, a movement was born, which has powerfully impacted hundreds of thousands of people around the world. It's NOT a fast from food, but a fast from wrong mindsets and thoughts that keep us limited and defeated.

Just as a butterfly is designed by God to fly, so are you! However, the butterfly can only emerge in its beautiful color and magnificent wings after it has been transformed within the warm cocoon of its Creator. What starts as a caterpillar is miraculously transformed into one of the most beautiful creatures God has ever made.

This Fast From Wrong Thinking devotional is your cocoon. As you wrap your mind in God's thoughts over the next 40 days, you too will be miraculously transformed, and you will *begin to fly!*

This is exactly the miraculous metamorphosis that God describes in Romans 12:2, when He says, *"Be transformed by the renewing of your mind."* That's what fasting from wrong thinking is all about. The Message Bible tells us that as you do this, *"You'll be changed from the inside out."*

The way we think controls our entire life. Our thoughts shape our words, actions, and habits. Our thoughts release God's potential in our lives or limit us from experiencing His best. The Bible says it best:

"For as a man thinks within, so is he . . ." (Proverbs 23:7)

Jesus said to take His yoke because it's easy and His burden is light. (Matthew 11:30) That's the grace of God. He did the heavy lifting, and now, our job is to enter into His rest. This is accomplished when you begin to believe what God has already provided. That's what this journey is all about. It will awaken you to His work of GRACE in your life! You will be amazed at just how easy this will be.

It's time for you to take control of your life by taking control of your thoughts. It's time to stop living below your privileges and rights as a child of God.

I can tell you from my own experience and the amazing testimonies of others that what follows on these pages will be the catalyst for a life beyond your greatest dreams. Are you ready to eliminate the mindsets that have limited and confined you? Ready to awaken the unlimited possibilities of God?

Then let's go!

Gregory Dickow

DAY 1

"I Can't Change."

Just as a butterfly is designed by God to soar, so are you! However, the butterfly can only emerge in its beautiful color and magnificent wings after it has been transformed within the warm cocoon of its Creator!

This *Fast From Wrong Thinking* is your cocoon. As you wrap your mind in God's thoughts over the next 40 days, you too will be miraculously transformed!

Ready to fly? Let's go!

Today we're fasting from the thought that says, **"I Can't Change."**

We've all felt at times that we can't change a certain habit or a weakness in our lives. We often feel "confined" by whatever has previously "defined" us. But, as we change our mindsets regarding **WHO** we are and what God has given us, **ANYTHING** can change. Today a new hope will be born in you!

LET'S CHANGE IT TODAY

1. **Awaken to God's grace.** His grace empowers us to change, to break a habit, or to be free from our past. The river of grace is always flowing. Just step into it and receive!

2. **Believe that the power to change is a GIFT.**
2 Timothy 2:25 says God grants "repentance" or
"the power to change" AS A GIFT.

3. **All change begins by believing you are loved by
God.** Romans 2:4b says, "Don't you realize that it is
God's loving kindness that is trying to lead you to
change the way you think and act?" (GWT)

4. Notice, in that verse, that **His love and kindness
changes the way we think; THEN they change the
way we act.** All lasting change begins by surrender-
ing your thought life to the Word of God.

5. **Believe in the process that leads to progress.** Don't
worry if it doesn't happen right away. Jesus touched
the blind man once, in Mark 8, and then touched
him a second time, before he was completely healed.
I believe these next 40 days are going to be your
SECOND touch from Jesus.

6. **Redefine yourself ONLY as what God says about
you.** Disconnect from the past definition of your
habits, traits, and limitations. You are being changed
into His image.

THINK IT AND SAY IT

God has given me the gift to change. My habits, emotions, and life will change by changing the way I think. I submit to the process of renewing my mind, and I expect divine progress. I refuse to accept past definitions and limitations of myself. As I embrace God's view of me, through His Word, I am being changed into His image, in Jesus' Name!

Scriptures

- Titus 2:12

- 2 Timothy 2:25

- James 1:6

- Romans 12:2

- Mark 8:22–26

- 2 Corinthians 3:18

Day 2
"I Feel Powerless."

When we feel powerless over our past, we feel guilty. When we feel powerless over our future, we feel afraid. When we feel powerless over the present, we feel depressed. And when we feel like the people or circumstances of our lives just won't change, we feel angry.

A sense of powerlessness is the root of all negative emotions.

The thought that there's not much we can do about the economy, or our weight, or the allergies we grew up with forces us to accept and tolerate a mediocre and weak life.

LET'S CHANGE IT TODAY

1. **Take inventory!** God has NOT given you a spirit of fear; but POWER, LOVE, and a SOUND MIND.

2. **Believe that power is in you.** Ephesians 3:20 says, "God is able to do exceedingly abundantly above all we can ask or think according to the power that is at work within you." There is power in you that enables God to do beyond what you can ask or think!

3. **THINK AND ASK BIG!** Give God something to work with, because He can do beyond. We have to at least give Him a base to begin with.

4. **Recognize the Holy Spirit in you.** Acts 1:8 says, "You shall receive power when the Holy Spirit comes upon you . . ." This power (*dunamis* = *dynamite*) is already in you. Romans 8:11 says, "The very same Spirit that raised Jesus from the dead lives IN YOU."

5. **Take the limits off. Don't limit God.** Psalm 78:41 says that the children of Israel limited the Lord because they did not remember His power (verse 42). We free God's Hand to bless when we remember His previous blessings.

6. **EXPECT!** Never underestimate the power of expectation. Expect God's power to strengthen you today. Expect to be led by His Spirit.

THINK IT AND SAY IT

I have POWER in my life right now. Through the Holy Spirit in me, I have the power to overcome temptation, the power to change my life for the better, the power to be healed, the power to forgive, and the power to speak God's Word and see His promises show up in my life. I will think big and ask big, and therefore the POWER OF GOD'S SPIRIT WITHIN ME will bring it to pass in my life, in Jesus' Name!

Scriptures

- 2 Timothy 1:7
- Ephesians 3:20
- Acts 1:8
- Romans 8:11

Day 3

"I Am Afraid."

Fear is at the root of just about every negative thing that happens in our lives. We're afraid of failing; afraid of being alone or rejected; afraid of running out of money; afraid that people will let us down; afraid that we won't find a spouse or the one we found will leave us.

All fear is rooted in the core belief that God's Word won't work. For example, the fear of not having enough is rooted in the fear that Philippians 4:19 isn't true. If you believe that "God will supply all your needs according to His riches . . ." then fear leaves.

LET'S CHANGE IT TODAY

1. **Meditate on the fact that God's Word is true.** In John 17:17, Jesus said, "Thy Word is truth." What God says is fact—whether you feel it, see it, or have ever experienced it.

2. **Consider God's track record.** 1 Kings 8:56 says, ". . . Every word has come true of all His good promise . . ." (NLV). Fear leaves when you can rely on something that can't fail. God has never failed to fulfill His promises. There are over 1000 predictions or prophecies in the Bible—promises that God

made before they happened. The chances of merely 17 of these coming to pass are 1 out of 450 billion x 1 billion x 1 trillion! Yet, not one of these promises has failed.

3. **Accept the truth that what we fear comes upon us.** In Job 3:25, Job feared that his children would curse God, and that's what happened. When you realize fear has the power to produce negative results, you stop dabbling in it. When a child learns what fire can do, he no longer plays with matches!

4. **Perfect love casts out fear.** (1 John 4:18) Flood your mind with thoughts of love—God's love for you, and what He was willing to do to rescue you. If He would die for you, while you were in sin and separated from God, there's just nothing He wouldn't do for you! Think on that, and fear will leave.

5. **There is a promise from God's Word for every need you will ever experience.** In fact, there are over 7000 promises in the Bible. That's 7000 solutions to life's problems! For example, there is a promise of protection in Psalm 91:1–12, which delivers you from the fear of evil, sickness, or tragedy.

6. **Pause and dwell on the fact that God is with you.** God's presence is the secret to a fear-free life. Ultimately, all fear is a sense of God's absence or our

separation from God. By contrast, a sense of God's presence delivers us from fear. Hebrews 10:19 says, We are in His presence by the blood of Jesus." You are in His presence now—therefore, fear not!

THINK IT AND SAY IT

God's Word is true, whether I feel it or not. He has kept all of His promises and has never failed. I am in God's presence by the blood of Jesus; therefore, because He is with me, I will fear no evil! God loves me perfectly, which casts out all my fear. I have power, love, and a sound mind, in Jesus' Name!

Scriptures

- John 17:15–19

- 1 Kings 8:56

- 1 John 4:17–19

- Psalm 91:1–12

Day 4

"I Don't Feel Loved."

We have embarked upon the most significant journey of our lives: fasting from wrong thinking. And today's thought is probably the most important one any of us ever deal with at a deep level.

Today we are fasting from the thought that says, **"I don't feel loved."**

The number-one need in every human life is to be loved. Yet sadly, so few actually enjoy a life where they actually feel loved.

LET'S CHANGE IT TODAY

1. **God's not mad at you, He's mad about you!** Dispel the myth of an angry God. He poured out His wrath on Jesus while on the cross, so He could pour His love on you forever. "God is love." (1 John 4:8)

2. **Our feelings follow our thoughts.** Flood your mind with the thought, "My Heavenly Father tenderly loves me!" (John 16:27 AMP) You and God are inseparable. Nothing can separate you from Him or His love. Believe this with every fiber in your being!

3. **Recognize your value.** The value of a piece of art is not determined by the cost to make it, but rather by *how much someone would pay to have it.* God paid for us with the blood of Jesus. That makes us as valuable to God, as Jesus Himself! You are priceless!

4. **You don't have to earn something God has already given.** He loves you. That can't be earned. It is a gift from God. (John 3:16) Accept it. Your value is not determined by what you've done or not done. Just *be loved.*

5. **Reject the voices of rejection.** Look in the mirror and tell yourself that you are chosen by God, accepted, and outrageously loved by your Heavenly Father!

6. **Know your calling.** By this, I'm not referring to your calling to serve in ministry or your profession. I'm talking about what God calls you. He calls you *His beloved* continually in the Bible. Do a word search. You are His beloved. So, *be loved!*

THINK IT AND SAY IT

God is not mad at me; He's mad about me! I am outrageously loved by Him! His anger lasted for a moment on the cross, but His love and favor are for a lifetime! My Heavenly Father tenderly loves me. Therefore, I will feel His love today! He continually calls me His beloved. Nothing can separate me from His love. I am valuable and priceless to Him. I am as valuable to God as Jesus is. I receive His love by faith, in Jesus' Name!

Scriptures

- 1 John 4:8–10

- Romans 8:37–39

- Colossians 1:10–12

- Ephesians 1:3–6

Day 5

"Happiness Is So Hard To Find."

Today we are fasting from the thought that says, **"Happiness is so hard to find."**

There is no higher or deeper desire in the heart of mankind than happiness. It is the single most intoxicating emotion that drives every decision and pursuit of mankind.

People have been looking for happiness—trying to buy it, trade for it, or discover it—since time began. But it's not hard to find.

LET'S CHANGE IT TODAY

1. **You don't have to find happiness.** It will find you! Jesus tells us in Matthew 6:33 that as we seek His kingdom ". . . all these things will be added to you." Expect happiness to be added to you as you put His kingdom first. How do you do that? Start each day by planting the seed of God's Word in your life.

2. **Happy is the man who does not condemn himself.** Refuse to tolerate condemnation another second of your life. Romans 8:1 says, *"there is no condemnation."* Believe that Jesus freed you from condemnation, and happiness will come!

GREGORY DICKOW MINISTRIES 25

3. **Treat unhappiness as a signal to trust God.** Jeremiah 17:7 says, "Happy is the man that trusts in the Lord." Declare that you trust Him today!

4. **The supreme happiness in life is the ASSURANCE that you are loved.** You can be sure God loves you—no matter what. Nothing can separate you from His love. Think on that.

5. **God will help you be happy today.** Psalm 146:5 says, "Happy is he whose help and hope are in the Lord." Ask for His help today. Ask Him for hope today. Believe you have received it, and joy will come.

6. **In His presence is *fullness* of joy.** Be mindful that you are in His presence *now*, by the blood of Jesus. And the Holy Spirit lives in you! It will change your view of life.

THINK IT AND SAY IT

I have the fullness of joy and happiness in life because I am in God's presence, and the Holy Spirit lives in me. I walk in the supreme happiness of life, knowing that I am loved by God. I refuse to condemn myself because there is no condemnation in Christ Jesus. God will always help me, and my hope is in Him. Therefore, I am happy, in Jesus' Name!

Scriptures

- Mark 4:26–29
- Jeremiah 17:7–8
- Romans 8:38–39
- Psalm 146:5–10

Day 6

"I Feel Anxious."

Today we are fasting from the thought that says, **"I Feel Anxious."**

All of us deal with anxiety at various times in our lives. Some of the symptoms of anxiety include heart palpitations, tension, fatigue, nausea, chest pain, shortness of breath, stomach aches, and headaches. You don't have to live this way.

LET'S CHANGE IT TODAY

1. **Treat anxiety as a signal rather than a condition.** It is a signal to pray, and prayer will change your outlook of the thing you are facing.

2. **More praying about it = less worrying about it.** James 5:16 says, *"The prayer of the righteous avails much."* Stop trying to SUBTRACT the anxiety. Instead, just ADD *prayer* the moment you feel it, and anxiety will leave!

3. **When panic attacks, attack back!** How do you attack anxiety and panic? You speak God's Word out of your mouth.

4. **It's not your fault!** Embrace this truth. Don't blame yourself for feeling anxious. It's the thief that comes to steal, kill, and destroy. Stop beating yourself up when you feel anxiety. Instead, beat up on the enemy by speaking God's Word.

5. **Remember your value.** Because you are so valuable in God's eyes, He will care for you. Yes, He values you, because He paid for you with the blood of Jesus! Worry and anxiety lose their power.

6. **Breathe praise to God.** *"Let everything that has breath, praise the Lord"* (Psalm 150:6). Experts agree that breathing literally helps manage anxiety. But when you BREATHE praise to God, you don't just manage anxiety, you MASTER it.

THINK IT AND SAY IT

Anxiety has lost its power over me. When I feel anxious, it is a signal to pray and praise God. When I add prayer, anxiety is subtracted. Because I am so valuable to God, I know that He will take care of me. I attack panic by speaking the Word of God. The Prince of Peace lives inside of me, therefore, I have peace guarding my heart and mind. I breathe praise to God today, in Jesus' Name!

Scriptures

- Philippians 4:6–7
- James 5:16–18
- Proverbs 18:21
- Matthew 6:25–31

Day 7
The "Problem-Focused" Mentality

Today we're fasting from what I call the **"problem-focused" mentality.** The problem-focused mentality just sees and reports the problem.

LET'S CHANGE IT TODAY

1. **Never be satisfied with just recognizing a problem.** There are enough critics and complainers in the world. The world needs solution-minded people, not just those who can report a problem.

2. **We are compensated in life for the problems we solve, not the problems we merely recognize.** In Genesis 41, Joseph not only recognized the famine coming, but he offered a solution for the famine. As a result, he became the most powerful man in the world. Even Pharaoh bowed his heart to Joseph and recognized his power.

3. **Love math!** What do I mean? Mathematics is a great discipline because it proves there is a solution to every problem. Whether you liked math in school, we need to get this: there is a solution to *everything*. Ask for it.

4. **You have the mind of Christ.** With His mind, you will find His solutions. With every problem man created, God had a solution. And you have His mind!

5. **Lean on the Holy Spirit.** As we are led by the Holy Spirit and pray in the Holy Spirit, we bring His solutions into our situation. Romans 8:26–27 says, *"the Spirit helps our weaknesses. For we do not know how to pray as we should, but the Spirit Himself makes intercession for us . . . according to the will [solutions] of God."*

6. **Stop talking about the problem and start talking to it.** Jesus said, "If you shall say to this mountain, be removed and cast into the sea, and do not doubt . . . it shall obey you." Use your mouth to move the problem.

THINK IT AND SAY IT

I believe that God will give me the interpretations of life's problems and that He will bless me with wisdom and answers. I believe there is a solution to every problem because I have the mind of Christ. I welcome the Holy Spirit to pray through me and bring God's will and solutions to my life and to the lives of those around me, in Jesus' Name!

Scriptures

- Genesis 45:8
- Romans 8:26–27
- Mark 11:23–24

Day 8

"It's Impossible."

Today we are fasting from the thought that says, **"It's impossible."**

Jesus said, "All things are possible to him who believes". What is in your life today that you have given up on or considered impossible? Whatever it is (provided it's legal!), don't ever give up. *Never, never, never give up.*

One Easter weekend, a major political story broke in America. The *New York Times* asked me, "Since this story is so big, will you be speaking about it at church on Easter?" "It certainly is a big story," I responded, "But SOMEONE RISING FROM THE DEAD IS EVEN BIGGER!" They then asked what I would specifically say about it. I answered, "If a man can rise from the dead, anything is possible!"

So today, let's fast from the thought that says, **"It's impossible."**

LET'S CHANGE IT TODAY

1. **Think about the resurrection every day.** This reveals the miraculous power of God to do anything! We tend to save these thoughts for Easter, but we need to think about the resurrection *all the time.* It awakens hope and faith in the possibilities of God.

2. **Stop thinking or saying, "I can't believe that."**
Cynicism and skepticism have filled our culture. We
need to get out of the habit of questioning and doubting the possibility of things. When you think there is
no way, remember that JESUS IS THE WAY!

3. **Deal with the real problem.** It's not whether God
will help. It's whether we believe. The man with the
demon-possessed son came to Jesus and said, "If you
can do anything, help us . . ." Jesus responded and
said, "If you can believe . . ." See? It's not whether
God can do it. It's whether we can believe it. And
remember that faith comes from hearing God's
Word.

4. **You are bigger than a mountain.** Believe that your
words move mountains. Matthew 17:20 says, "You
shall say to this mountain, 'Remove from here to
there,' and it shall remove; and nothing shall be
impossible to you." That's big! You're big!

5. **Meditate on people who had an impossible turn-
around.** Abraham was 99 years old when he had a
son. Sarah was 90! Moses parted the Red Sea. The
list goes on and on. Find those people in the Bible and
fill your mind with their testimonies. Hebrews 12:1
says, "We have a great cloud of witnesses surround-
ing us . . ." If it could happen for them, it can happen
for you, and *it will*.

6. God CAN'T lie. There is only ONE THING in this world that is impossible: it's impossible for God to lie. Don't throw away your confidence in God's promises. He will fulfill them.

THINK IT AND SAY IT

All things are possible for me because I believe God's Word. All of His promises are possible because all His promises are "Yes"; and He can't lie. Jesus is the WAY when it seems like there is no way. Faith comes as I hear God's Word; and faith moves the impossible mountain as I speak God's Word today, in Jesus' Name!

Scriptures

- Mark 9:20–27

- Matthew 17:20

Day 9

"I Feel Like a Victim."

Today we're fasting from the thought that says, **"I feel like a victim."**

Viktor Frankl survived the Nazi death camp at Auschwitz by defining ultimate freedom as the ability "to choose one's attitude in any given set of circumstances."

The worst prison in the world is the one we put ourselves in—our minds.

LET'S CHANGE IT TODAY

1. **No one can keep you in your current situation, except you.** We must begin TODAY to accept total responsibility to become victors, not victims. You are MORE than a conqueror—more than a victor.

2. **People may have had something to do with how you got in the situation, but only YOU can decide whether you stay in the situation.**

3. **The *victim* mentality ends when we TAKE FULL RESPONSIBILITY for our attitude and direction in life.** Deuteronomy 30:15,19 says, "See, I have set before you this day, life and prosperity and death and adversity . . . so choose life, that both you and your

descendants might LIVE (the victorious, abundant, God kind of life)."

4. **Ask the Holy Spirit to help you. Full responsibility doesn't mean that we're in it alone.** God is on our side, and He will help us. It's natural to look for help—but let's get it from God. John 16:13 says, "The Holy Spirit is *our Helper!*" When you have His help, you don't need to blame anyone for anything! We blame when we feel helpless—but we're NOT!

5. **Understand the root word of responsibility is response.** We may not be able to control everything that others do to us, but we can control our RESPONSE. In our response, lies our freedom and our growth.

6. **Don't give away your power.** We give away our power to live in victory, health, and success—when we allow others to determine how we RESPOND. We have the power to forgive, the power to recover, and the power to overcome anything. When we blame others, we give away that power to them.

7. **TAKE CHARGE OVER WHAT GOD HAS GIVEN YOU.** The master said to the servant who hid his talent, "Why didn't you at least invest my money so I could have received interest?" (Matthew 25:24–27) He blamed the master and excused himself. As

a result, he fell to the temptation of resentment and fear. He lost everything because he had a victim mentality.

THINK IT AND SAY IT

No one can keep me down! I am not a victim. I am a victor. I take full responsibility for my responses in life—my attitudes and my decisions. Holy Spirit, I am asking for your help. You live in me, and you are my Helper! I refuse to give away my power by blaming others. I take responsibility for my thoughts, my actions, and my REACTIONS. I abandon the idea that my situation is the fault of anyone else. I am an overcomer. I am more than a conqueror, in Jesus' Name!

Scriptures

- Romans 8:37

- Deuteronomy 30:15–19

- John 16:13

Day 10

"I'm Feeling Offended."

Today we are fasting from the thought that says, **"I'm feeling offended."**

We all know what's it like to be treated wrongly or unfairly and to be talked about or lied about. It's easy to become offended and feel that we have the right to feel that way. But this is a destructive trap.

LET'S CHANGE IT TODAY

1. **Being offended traps *you*.** *Skandalon* (offense) is the trigger of a well-baited trap. When an animal touches the trigger of a snare, it snaps down on him and he is trapped. When you are offended, you are the one caught in the trap. By thinking and knowing this, it will empower you to stay out of the traps.

2. **Being offended comes from self-righteousness.** We think, "How could they do that to me? I would never have done that!" But we have all sinned. Embrace humility with the sure knowledge that you have failed, too. And *offense* loses its grip on you.

3. **You can't afford to *pay attention!*** 1 Corinthians 13:5 (Amplified Bible) says, *"Love (God's love in us)*

is not touchy or fretful or resentful." Why? "Because it **pays no attention** to a suffered wrong." We get offended when we pay attention to the wrong we have suffered. Stop paying attention. It's too expensive.

4. **Take back control.** We let others control us when we pay attention to what they did to us. What God did FOR you is greater than what others have done TO you. Focus on what God has done for you.

5. **Express UP, not OUT.** Fully express your anger and hurt out loud to God. Tell Him how much it hurt. Forgive the offender (out loud to God), whether you feel anything or not; and ask Him to heal you.

6. **NOTHING CAN OFFEND YOU!** How is that possible? Psalm 119:165 says, *"Those who love the Word have great peace, and nothing offends them."* One of the meanings of the Greek word for "love" is "attachment". Attach yourself to what God says, and you'll detach from the power of what others have done or said to you. That's what it means to love God's Word.

THINK IT AND SAY IT

I am free from being offended. I am free from the emotions of offense, bitterness, and the right to feel mad. I will not be trapped by those feelings. I love God's Word. I attach myself to what He said and did. I refuse to pay attention to the wrong done to me. I forgive and release those that have hurt me. I express my feelings to God, and I am healed, in Jesus' Name!

Scriptures

- 1 Corinthians 13:5–8

- Psalm 119:165

Day 11

"I Feel Depressed."

Today we're fasting from the thought that says, **"I feel depressed."**

We have all felt it at times. Depression is now the leading cause of disability in the world. So often, depression is anger turned inward at ourselves for our shortcomings and mistakes.

Perhaps you've thought: "Life's a drag; what's the use; I'll never be happy." These thoughts are designed to rob you of the joy and confidence that produces supernatural strength in our lives.

LET'S CHANGE IT TODAY

1. **Stop condemning yourself.** Condemnation is a mindset that robs you of joy and peace. Romans 14:22 says, *"Happy is the man who does not condemn himself . . ."* Don't condemn yourself because God doesn't condemn you.

2. **God's still working on you!** Philippians 1:6 tells us to lighten up on ourselves. He began a good work in you; He'll finish it! Trust God that you're making progress. You're not standing still.

3. **Tap into the power of believing.** 1 Peter 1:8 says: "*. . . though you do not see Him now, you BELIEVE in Him, and are filled with inexpressible and glorious joy.*" Believe the promise of God regardless of what you feel, and depression will begin to leave.

4. **REJECT Shame.** Jesus took your shame on the cross. No matter what you feel or what you've done. We are all dealing with something. If you feel darkness, remember: God is with you, even in the valley.

5. **Surround yourself with positive people.** Positive thinking and speaking are contagious, just as negative thinking is. Surround yourself only with those who create an atmosphere of victory with their attitude and words.

6. **Remember, you are not helpless.** Thoughts of helplessness bring depression. The Holy Spirit is our Helper. He has not left you alone and He will never leave you alone.

7. **Depression comes from a sense of powerlessness.** You have the power to pray and receive the answer—this sense of power brings joy.

I will never be depressed another day in my life. I decide to stop condemning myself and beating myself up for my shortcomings. I believe God is working in me every day.

I am not a negative thinker. I am positive. God is for me, with me and in me, therefore depression cannot stay. I am not helpless because I have the Holy Spirit living in me. I command every ounce of depression to loose me and let me go. I command it to be removed and cast into the sea, in Jesus' Name!

Scriptures

- Philippians 1:6

- Psalm 23:4

- John 14:16–18

- John 16:23–24

"I Can't Shake My Past."

Today we are fasting from the thought that says, **"I can't shake my past."** Often our past is what limits us and keeps us defeated.

LET'S CHANGE IT TODAY

1. **Meet the new you.** You truly are a new creation—if you are in Christ. The old has passed away. Your past is over!

2. **God will use your past.** Live in Romans 8:28. All things, including your past, work for your GOOD! While your past is over, God can still make it work to your advantage. Believe that.

3. **You are more than a conqueror.** That means your past doesn't conquer you! You have conquered it, by being in Christ. You're the head and not the tail! See yourself that way, and your past loses its grip on you.

4. **You are *not guilty*.** No matter how guilty you were, you have been pronounced by Jesus as "NOT GUILTY." Jesus has washed all your sins away. (Romans 8:34) That's how God sees you. Now, you can start seeing yourself that way.

5. **You *can* shake it off!** In Acts 28:5, Paul shook off a serpent from his hand. And you have the power to do so as well. Nothing can harm you anymore—not even your past mistakes or shortcomings. Shake it off by speaking to it!

6. **Have a funeral for regret.** Kiss regret goodbye. Have a burial service for whatever is nagging you. Take 20 seconds and pray this funeral prayer: "Lord, I thank you that this sin or mistake of my past is dead and gone. You have removed it and forgotten it, therefore so do I! I shake it off and commit it to You." And thus concludes this funeral service for your past!

THINK IT AND SAY IT

I am a new creation in Christ Jesus; and no matter how bad my past is, it's not only forgiven—it's washed away! I am more than a conqueror, and I will not be pushed around by memories or people from my past. Because of the blood of Jesus, I am not guilty. I shake off my past. I declare it is over, and I expect God will turn my situation around for good in some miraculous way, in Jesus' Name!

Scriptures

- 2 Corinthians 5:17
- Romans 8:28
- Romans 8:37
- Romans 8:34
- Hebrews 8:12

Day 13

"I Haven't Done Enough."

Today we are fasting from the thought that says, "**I haven't done enough.**"

When things don't go our way, we sometimes have this nagging thought that we're not holy enough or haven't prayed enough to qualify us for God's blessing or favor.

LET'S CHANGE IT TODAY

1. **We get what Jesus deserves.** Romans 8:17 tells us that we are joint heirs with Jesus Christ. His inheritance is ours. 1 John 4:17 says, *"As He is, so are we in this world."* This is the great exchange! We deserved the curse, but instead we get His blessing.

2. **Be covenant-minded.** You have a covenant with God. A covenant is a contract—in this case, a contract that is guaranteed by the shed blood of Jesus Christ.

3. **Be grace-minded.** Grace is when God gives us what we don't deserve. Hebrews 4:16 says, *"Therefore, let us draw near with confidence [boldly] to the throne of grace, so that we may receive mercy and find grace to help in time of need."*

4. **Have confidence in God, not in yourself** (1 John 3:20–21). Confidence and faith enable God to answer prayers in our lives.

5. **Reject condemnation.** It is our heart that condemns us for our mistakes and shortcomings. When we feel condemned, we lose confidence, and then we believe we can't receive anything from God.

6. **Accept your freedom in Christ.** There is now NO condemnation for those who are in Christ! (Romans 8:1)

7. **Stop beating yourself up about what you haven't done.** We often punish ourselves with self-condemnation. We will *never* do enough for God. That's why Jesus did it all. He *paid* for sin, sickness, the curse, and our failure. *Our work, our battle, is to simply believe.*

THINK IT & SAY IT

I let go of the mindset that tells me I'm not holy enough, or I haven't done enough to receive answered prayers. I receive His promises by faith. I am a joint heir with Jesus Christ. I expect to get what He deserves, not what I deserve. The throne of His grace is always open! His river of lavish love-gifts are always flowing towards me! I receive His grace, freely and lavishly, in Jesus' Name!

Scriptures

- Romans 8:17
- Hebrews 8:12–13
- Hebrews 4:15
- 1 John 3:20–21
- Romans 8:1

Day 14

"That's Just the Way I Am."

Today we are fasting from the thought that says: "**That's just the way I am.**"

One of the things that limits us and keeps us defeated is the opinion we have of ourselves. Over time, we begin to accept a version of ourselves that isn't God's version. We also accept other people's stigmas of us: "He's shy"; "She's self-absorbed"; "He's all talk"; "She's not the sharpest knife in the drawer."

We often end up living up to the very opinions and expectations that others have had of us because we've been conditioned to do so.

LET'S CHANGE IT TODAY

1. **You are a work of art—a work in progress.** God is the potter and we are the clay. (Jeremiah 18:1–6) God is working on you to make you what He wants you to be. Trust the Artist to make a masterpiece. Be flexible and adaptable. See yourself as a GOOD work in progress.

2. **Withhold judgment of yourself (or others).** Philippians 1:6 says, *"He who began a GOOD work in you will complete it until the day of Jesus Christ."* Don't

prejudge what your capacity is or what your potential is. He's only just begun!

3. **God doesn't throw you out.** HE NEVER GIVES UP ON YOU. Jeremiah 18:4 says, "The clay was marred, so He made it again." He didn't discard it. He made it again. Thank God! He's re-making you!

4. **You are changing as you are reading this!** Whatever flaws you have, they are not the final sentence. You are NOW being transformed to the very image of Jesus!

5. **EMBRACE the GRACE!** In 1 Corinthians 15:10, Paul said "I AM what I AM by the grace of God." It's God's grace IN YOU that is making you what you are. You are not a composite of your parents' mistakes, your mistakes, or others' opinions of you. You're awesome! You are a work of God's grace.

6. **Take another look!** The Bible is a mirror that reflects what God and you really look like! We are everything God says we are. As Jesus is, so are we in this world! (1 John 4:17) THAT'S the way you are!

THINK IT AND SAY IT

I am unlimited in my ability to grow and change. God is the potter and I am the clay. I am what God says I am. He began a good work in me, and He will finish it. He is making me into something GOOD. I am His workman-ship—His work of art. He's good at this and has been doing it for a long time! I am not in bondage to my weaknesses and former limitations. They do not define me. Every day and every moment that passes is making me more and more like Jesus!

Scriptures

- Jeremiah 18:1–6

- 2 Corinthians 3:18

- 1 Corinthians 15:10

- 1 John 4:17

Day 15

"God Is Far From Me."

Today we are fasting from the thought that says, **"God is far from me."**

We must learn to not only discern between right and wrong, but we must discern between *right* and *almost right*.

It's *almost right* to ask God to come down and help us. It sounds holy. It sounds humble. But you will truly be free when you discover, *He is already here. Emmanuel* means, "God WITH us". When Jesus came to the earth, He put an end to the separation between God and man.

Separation between us and God and us is a myth. The devil wants us to believe it to keep us powerless. We were separated from God through our sin (Isaiah 59:2), but Jesus *took away* the sin through His blood. Therefore, the moment we are born again, there is *no separation* anymore. We sometimes feel that He is so far away, but He is not. He is here. He is there. He is everywhere we are.

LET'S CHANGE IT TODAY

1. **Psalm 46:1 says, *"He is an ever-present help in times of trouble."*** Wow! You have to love this thought. Have you ever had times of trouble? But notice, He is ever-present. Then, it says, *help* in times

of trouble. It is His ever-presence that brings us help in times of trouble.

2. **Take Him at His Word.** Jesus said in Matthew 28:20, *"Lo, I am with you always; even to the end of the age."* There is no way to misinterpret this verse. Jesus is with YOU always. That has to warm your heart and comfort you.

3. **Christianity is not a life of attainment, but a life of recognition.** Philemon 1:6 says, *"Your faith might become effective, through the **acknowledgment** of those things which are already in you, in Christ Jesus."* Many people focus on attaining God's presence and God's blessing. But the Scripture is clear: Acknowledge. Recognize He is already in you. His gifts are already in you!

4. **Christianity is not about us *finding* God.** It's that Jesus came and found us, spilled His blood to cleanse us from all unrighteousness, took us into His arms, and breathed His very Spirit into us. Now He lives in every person that has accepted Him as their Savior and Lord. Romans 8:11 tells us that the Spirit of God lives in us!

5. **Resist the temptation to pray, "God, come down and help me," or "Send Your Spirit."** He has already come. He has already sent His Spirit. Our

battle is to believe this whether we feel His presence or not. He is in us!

6. **It's not us living *for* God. It's us living *from* God.** Galatians 2:20 says, *"It is no longer I who live, but Christ lives in me."*

THINK IT AND SAY IT

I am not separated from God in any way. He is an ever-present help in my time of trouble. His ever-presence brings me help! I recognize that He is already in me. That's what makes my faith work.

God is not far off. He is right here, right now. I am surrounded by His love and enveloped in His presence. Therefore, I am not afraid. I am not trying to live FOR God; I am living FROM Him. His power is in me. His presence is in me. His love is in me. And nothing can ever separate me from the love of God, which is in Christ Jesus, my Lord! Amen.

Scriptures

- Psalm 46:1

- Matthew 28:20

- Philemon 6

- Galatians 2:20

- Psalm 139:7-9

Small Thinking

Today we are fasting from **small thinking.** THIS IS GOING TO CHANGE EVERYTHING!

Small thinking produces small living. If we set up small expectations for our lives, that's what we'll get. The problem with that mindset is that God is bigger than we ever imagined, and has bigger plans for us than we've ever dreamed. **Time to ditch small thinking!**

LET'S CHANGE IT TODAY

1. **Your god is too small! Everything changes when we LET GO OF A SMALL GOD. How big is your God?** Scientists estimate there are over 100 billion galaxies, and 100 billion stars in each of them! And God created them and calls them all by name. He's BIG.

2. **How big is He?** He's big enough to take away the sin of the world; to allow us to make mistakes without punishment; to put great dreams in human hearts; and big enough to not have to threaten us to accept Him. **He's a BIG BIG GOD!**

3. **Think big!** Renew your mind to God's language. For example: "Ask for the nations" (Psalm 2); "Speak to the mountain" (Mark 11); "Your descendants shall

be as numerous as the stars" (Genesis 15); "You shall possess the land" (Numbers 13), and so on. God uses *big* language and gives us *big* dreams!

4. **Ask big! Get your Jabez on! He prayed: Lord, bless me indeed. Enlarge my territory . . ." Ask Him that today . . ." and God granted his request."** Ephesians 3:20 says, "God is able to do exceeding abundantly beyond all that we can ask or think." Start asking and thinking the way God says to.

5. **Never stop dreaming and envisioning a better life.** In Acts 2:17 God says, *"In the last days I will pour out my Spirit upon all people. Your young men will see visions, and your old men will dream dreams."* You see? He says, *"Old men will dream dreams"* because even as we get older, we are not supposed to stop dreaming! God wants you to keep dreaming no matter what!

6. **Take your seat!** What do I mean? God has seated us with Jesus Christ in heavenly places (Ephesians 2:6). We have been given a divine authority and divine point of view. That's how we need to look at life— from our position, seated above all limitations!

7. **Imprint this on your heart and mind: *royalty destroys inferiority!*** Acquaint yourself with your new bloodline. You are royalty in Christ. This makes you reign over life (Romans 5:17). When you know

that you are made righteous and made royal by His blood, it makes you as confident and bold as a lion! Believe it!

THINK IT AND SAY IT

I give up small thinking. I let go of a small god. I agree with God's way of looking at things and God's language. I choose to think bigger and bigger every day, and to ask for the things God desires for me. I accept the visions and dreams that the Holy Spirit wants to give me; and I let go of all failure, disappointment, and fear-based thoughts, in Jesus' Name!

Scriptures

- Isaiah 40:26

- Ephesians 3:20

- Acts 2:17

- Ephesians 2:6

- Proverbs 28:1

"My Life Is Not That Special."

Today we are fasting from the thought that says, **"My life is not that special."**

Though hard to admit, this mentality is often under the surface of our lives. It's a mindset that hems us into a mediocre and boring existence.

LET'S CHANGE IT TODAY

1. **You have a destiny**. Believe it. Jeremiah 1:5 says, *"Before you were formed in your mother's womb, I knew you and destined you . . ."*

2. **Remember the song, *"You're just too good to be true. Can't take my eyes off of you?"*** This is what God is saying about you! Genesis 16:13a says, *"You are the God who sees me!"*

3. **You cannot go unnoticed.** Luke 8:47 says, *"Then, the woman, **seeing that she could not go unnoticed,** came trembling and fell at His feet."* You are chosen by God.

4. **Jesus is coming over!** Remember Zacchaeus climbing up a tree to see Jesus? In Luke 19:5, *"Jesus looked up and said to him, 'Zacchaeus, come down. I must stay*

at your house today.'" He wants to come to YOUR house today. YOU ARE THAT IMPORTANT TO HIM.

5. **You are the apple of the Father's eye.** Whoever touches you is touching the apple of God's eye. *You are God's greatest desire.* You bring Him great joy!

THINK IT AND SAY IT

I have a destiny. I am chosen by God. I cannot go unnoticed by Jesus. He sees me, and recognizes me, and calls me His own. He is coming over to my house because He loves me and considers me significant. I reject all feelings of insignificance and unimportance. I am the apple of His eye, in Jesus' Name!

Scriptures

- Luke 8:47

- Colossians 3:12

- Zechariah 2:8

- Zephaniah 3:17

"I Can't Stop."

Today we are fasting from the thought that says, **"I can't stop."**

Quitting a habit, a sin, or an addiction can be one of the hardest things in life; but it becomes easy when we realize Jesus not only died to forgive our sins; but also to give us power over sin and to free us from being in bondage to anything.

LET'S CHANGE IT TODAY

1. **Stop trying to stop.** Instead, just continue to fast from wrong thinking. Proverbs 23:7 says, *"As a man thinks, so is he."* Your thoughts will shape your decisions; your decisions will shape your actions; your actions will shape your habits.

2. **Awaken to the grace of God.** Romans 6:14 tells us that sin does not have dominion over us *". . . for we are not under the law but under grace."* Embrace the grace! It is the free, unearned, and undeserved love of God!

3. **Grace empowers.** Titus 2:11 says, *"It is the grace of God that enables and instructs us to resist and deny ungodliness."* Go to God's throne of grace right now and ask for His help.

4. **His yoke is easy.** You are yoked to Jesus. That means He will carry the weight of your struggle and walk you through it.

5. **Change happens *to* you, not *by* you.** Romans 12:2 says, "*Be* transformed." This is something that happens TO you, as you renew your mind to God's Word. It's happening to you right now as you fast from wrong thinking! And as you fill your mind with God's goodness, it LEADS you to "repentance" (which is: to change your thinking, Romans 2:4).

6. **"There ain't no can't."** (Quote from Mickey to Rocky in the movie, *Rocky II*) Get rid of "can't" from your vocabulary and your mindset. You *can* do all things through Christ.

7. **Stop beating yourself up about what you haven't done.** We often punish ourselves with self-condemnation. We will *never* do enough for God. That's why Jesus did it all. He *paid* for sin, the curse, and our failure. *Our job is to believe.*

THINK IT AND SAY IT

I am not under the bondage or control of any sin, habit, or problem in my life anymore. I am under the grace of God, giving me dominion over sin and temptation.

I am yoked to Jesus. Therefore, it is His strength that I walk in. As I renew my mind to the Word of God, I am being changed and transformed, in Jesus' Name!

Scriptures

- Romans 6:14

- Matthew 11:28–30

- Philippians 4:13

- Romans 2:4

"I Don't Have Enough."

Most people know the benefits of fasting from food, but fasting from wrong thinking has been an untapped treasure and force—until now! As you continue this amazing journey and tap into this power, you will be transformed!

Today we are fasting from the thought that says, **"I don't have enough."**

This is a mindset that says, "I don't have enough money. I don't have enough time. I don't have enough friends. I don't have enough education, etc."

These thoughts build an invisible fence that keeps you in the backyard of lack and deficiency.

LET'S CHANGE IT TODAY

1. **Believe in God's abundant provision.** Our God calls Himself: El Shaddai, the God of more than enough. We have more than enough of God living inside of us. Let's stop thinking in terms of *not enough* and start thinking in terms of *more than enough*.

2. **Think multiplication.** God said: Be fruitful and multiply. He is a multiplier, and so are you. Believe in the God of multiplication!

3. **Think apple orchard.** An apple seed becomes an apple orchard. One little seed becomes more than enough apples for a whole community! Believe in the power of a seed.

4. **Seed meets need.** Remember, even God cannot multiply a seed that you don't sow. Sow a seed.

5. **Be patient.** Farmers understand there is seed, time, and harvest. Don't forget that *time* is the connector between the seed and the harvest.

6. **God is not trying to get something *from* you; He's trying to get something *to* you.** Trust. Let go. As you let go of what you have in your hand, you are able to receive what God is trying to put in your hand! Give, and it will be given back to you in good measure.

THINK IT AND SAY IT

I always have enough, because Philippians 4:19 says, *"God shall supply ALL my needs, according to His riches."* I always have enough, because My God is more than enough. I believe that seeds meet needs. I am a sower, and therefore I am a reaper. God is a multiplier, and so am I.

I am called to be fruitful and multiply. God is multiplying every good seed that I have ever sown. As I give, He gives back to me good measure, pressed down, shaken together, and running over, in Jesus' Name!

Scriptures

- Romans 8:11
- Mark 4:26
- Genesis 8:22
- Luke 6:38
- Philippians 4:19

Day 20

"It's Just so Hard to be a Christian."

Today we are fasting from the thought that says, **"It's just so hard to be a Christian."**

We are going to break this mentality once and for all because it is the single most often misunderstood concept that is keeping believers defeated.

Jesus said to take His yoke because it's easy and His burden is light. That's the grace of God! He did the heavy lifting, and now our job is to enter into His rest.

LET'S CHANGE IT TODAY

1. **It's not hard to be something you already are.** Jesus made you a Christian, and there's nothing that can change that. You're a new creation! You are already more than a conqueror! You don't have to TRY to be a human. You are one! In the same way: You ARE a Christian!

2. **It is He who made us, and not we ourselves.** Selah—pause and think on that. HE MADE YOU A CHRISTIAN. And you can't undo what God has done.

3. **Jesus did it all.** When He said, *"It is finished,"* in John 19:30, He meant: "The debt is paid; the sentence is served; the victory is won! I did everything necessary for you to be saved and at peace." Now, just believe it.

4. **Start realizing "Christian" means "Christ-IN."** He is in you. It's *impossible* for you to fail at being a Christian, when the anointing (Christ) is at work within you.

5. **His yoke is easy.** Reverse your thinking. Think, "It's easy to be a Christian." His yoke is *easy*. His burden is *light*. You are yoked/connected/hitched to Him!

6. **Rest in the fact that you don't have to be perfect.** God is not holding you to a perfect standard. Jesus is your perfection. Just *rest* in this truth!

THINK IT AND SAY IT

It is easy to live the Christian life because God already made me more than a conqueror. Jesus did it all! His life is in me. His love is in me. His power is in me. His Spirit is in me. Therefore, I cannot fail as a Christian! I am not alone, and never will be. I am yoked to Him, and that's why I can enjoy my relationship WITH God, rather than strive to fulfill a duty FOR God. I am free, in Jesus' Name!

Scriptures

- 2 Corinthians 5:17

- Psalm 100:3

- 2 Corinthians 13:5

- Colossians 1:27

- Galatians 2:20

- Matthew 11:30

Day 21

"I Feel Like I've Failed."

Today we are fasting from the thought that says, **"I feel like I've failed,"** or **"I've failed in my relationship with God, in my faith, and in my life, etc."**

The feeling of failure can be disheartening and depressing. It can keep us in a cycle of defeat.

LET'S CHANGE IT TODAY

1. **You have comeback DNA in you.** Even in what seems like the worst situation, the same Spirit that raised Jesus from the dead lives in you. Expect your comeback! You have resurrection DNA in you!

2. **Falling isn't failing.** Proverbs 24:16 says, *"A righteous man falls seven times, but he rises again!"* You are righteous in Christ. See yourself as someone who rises up. When you've fallen, you have the right to get back up.

3. **Jesus gets His prayers answered.** And He is praying for you, that your faith would not fail. Luke 22:32 tells us that Jesus said to Peter (and to *you*), *"I have prayed for you, that your faith would not fail." **You are not going to fail.*** No shame! Get up.

4. **Jesus is turning TO you, not FROM you!** In Luke 22:61, Jesus turned TO Peter after he denied Him. He didn't turn FROM him. You are accepted! This acceptance transformed Peter's life after he hit rock bottom. God accepts you, just like He accepted Peter, even when you've failed.

5. **Even when you're doing poorly, God will NOT FAIL you.** He's going to make sure you make it. Your relationship with Him was His idea, not yours. He will finish what He started.

6. **In one moment, God can turn around years of apparent failure.** In Esther 9:1, God's people were about to be destroyed, but God suddenly delivered them. In only ONE DAY, the tables were turned, and God transformed certain defeat into total victory! If God could accomplish this for them, He will do it for you!

THINK IT AND SAY IT

I have comeback DNA in me! It's my new nature to always rise, even when I've fallen. I have the blood-bought right to get back up when I've failed! Jesus doesn't turn from me when I've fallen; He turns to me and prays for me. I cannot fail. He will not fail me. His love will never fail toward me. I am expecting God to turn my failures and frustrations around beginning today, in Jesus' Name!

Scriptures

- Proverbs 24:16
- Luke 22:32
- Philippians 1:6

"I Just Can't Forgive Myself."

Today we are fasting from the thought that says: **"I just can't forgive myself."**

Who hasn't thought that at one time or another? The devil would love to keep us in self-condemnation for the things we have done or failed to do. He knows it paralyzes us and prevents us from making the impact that God intended for us.

LET'S CHANGE IT TODAY

1. **Realize that we only deserve forgiveness because of the blood of Jesus.** It's not because our mistakes "never happened," or "it wasn't that bad". Give up rationalizations and excuses, and simply receive God's mercy and grace.

2. **It WAS THAT bad, but God is even MORE good!** James 2:13 says, *"Mercy triumphs over judgment."* His mercy toward you TRIUMPHS over your self-judgment. In Luke 22:34, Peter denied the Lord three times, and Jesus forgave him. Later, Peter preached the first sermon after Jesus rose from the dead, and 3000 people were saved in a day! Peter was able to forgive himself when he knew Jesus had accepted him. In the same way, you too, have been accepted

by God, no matter what you have done—simply by believing in His finished work on the cross.

3. **Give up your right to hold ANYTHING against yourself. God doesn't hold anything against you.** Forgiving yourself is simply AGREEING with God. His standard is absolute perfection, and He forgives you. Psalm 103:12 says, *"As far as east is from west, so far has He removed our transgressions from us."*

4. **Stop rehearsing what you did.** It's done. It's over. Now accept the second chance (or third or fourth . . .) that God offers. Philippians 3:13 says *"Forgetting what lies behind, and reaching forward . . ."* Reaching forward starts in your thought life.

5. **Believe that guilt doesn't come from God.** He doesn't impose guilt on you to try to get you to stop doing something. Romans 2:4 says, *"It is His goodness that draws us to repentance."* Since this guilt and shame doesn't come from God, there can be only one other source—the devil. James 4:7 says, *"Submit to God, resist the devil, and he will flee from you."*

6. **Give up the SELF-PUNISHMENT.** Some people think subconsciously: "I'll make myself feel bad to pay for what I've done." Why should we pay the price that has ALREADY been paid for what we've done wrong? Stop beating yourself up. By trying to "pay

for what we have done," we are doubting and insulting the very blood of Jesus that HAS PAID the price in full. Accept His free gift.

THINK IT AND SAY IT

I receive mercy today, because of the blood of Jesus. Though I didn't deserve it, God proclaims over me that I am "not guilty". Where I have failed, God's mercy triumphs over judgment.

I give up my mindset today to hold ANYTHING against myself. I deserve to be punished, but Jesus took THAT punishment for me. I forget what lies behind and press on, moving forward in my life with God, even though I feel like I have blown it beyond repair.

I reject this guilt and self-condemnation that the devil is trying to put on me. God is the God of second chances. I will no longer try to make myself feel bad to pay for what I've done. The price for what I did or failed at has been paid in full by Jesus' blood!

Scriptures

- Psalm 103:12

- Philippians 3:13

- Romans 2:4

- James 4:7

- Ephesians 1:7

Day 23

"I Tried to Forgive, but I Just Don't Feel It."

Today we're fasting from the thought that says, ***"I tried to forgive but I just don't feel it."***

Many people are held back in life because they are waiting for the feeling of forgiveness before they let go. In the meantime, unforgiveness continues its damage against them, while they wait for their feelings to change. Your feelings won't change until your thoughts do!

LET'S CHANGE IT TODAY

1. **Forgiveness is not a feeling.** It is a decision to GIVE it as a free gift. Whatever grudge, bitterness, or resentment that you have toward someone will not go away without a choice to "give it" as a gift.

2. **Forgive by faith.** 2 Corinthians 5:7 says, *"We live by faith; therefore we forgive by faith."* Never let your faith follow your feelings. Your feelings will catch up with your faith.

3. **Don't be fooled by the feelings of resentment or anger when they try to come back.** You'll be

tempted to think, "I don't feel anything, so nothing has changed. I guess I must not have really forgiven them." This is a lie! This is the thought you must fast from. The moment you forgive someone, as a choice, it's done, no matter what you feel.

4. **Believe and be thankful that you are free from the pain and consequences of unforgiveness.** Thank God that you are free and healed. As you do this EVERY TIME that you feel those feelings, you will feel less and less of the pain, until it completely vanishes away.

5. **Understand the meaning of the word: FOR—GIVE.** It simply means to GIVE, BEFORE. We need to "give" forgiveness, BEFORE the person apologizes, BEFORE they change, and most importantly BEFORE you feel anything. Just as faith works by believing God's promises BEFORE they show up (Mark 11:24–25), forgiveness works BEFORE you feel it. When you forgive BEFORE you feel good feelings about that person, you are living in the highest level of faith.

6. **Meditate on what God has done FOR you, rather than what people have done TO you.** Psalm 103:2–4 says, *"Bless the Lord O my soul and forget none of his benefits—He pardons all your iniquities, heals all your*

diseases, redeems your life from destruction, crowns you with loving-kindness and compassion." Think on these things.

THINK IT AND SAY IT

I accept that forgiveness is not a feeling. It's a decision. Beginning today, I expect the bitter feelings, the problems, and the unanswered prayers to change because of the choice I have made.

I forgive by faith, which means that as I act on the Word of God and declare my forgiveness out loud, I am walking in forgiveness, whether I feel something or not.

I am forgiven and I am a forgiver! I choose to forgive others (AND MYSELF), BEFORE they change, before they deserve it, and before I feel it. I focus on what God has done for me, rather than what others have done to me, and therefore, I am free. In Jesus' Name!

Scriptures

- 2 Corinthians 5:7

- Mark 11:24–25

- Psalm 103:2–4

"I Can't Control My Emotions."

Today we're fasting from the thoughts that say: **"I can't control my emotions."**

We all have emotions, but unfortunately sometimes THEY have us!

God created us to live with positive and healthy emotions. It's the negative ones that can harm our lives, our relationships, and our future. The idea that we are "victims" of our emotions because of our gender, our culture, our ethnicity, or our personality type, has to be eliminated.

LET'S CHANGE IT TODAY

1. **Our emotions are the result of our thoughts**. If you think sad thoughts, you will become sad. If you think joyful and faith-filled thoughts, you will become happy. As a man thinks within, so is he.

2. **Reject the belief that your emotions are the result of your culture, ethnicity, or gender.** Your culture may be more or less expressive of emotions, but we are all spiritual beings with the power to rule over our emotions with the Word of God.

3. **You have been given SELF-CONTROL.** It is in you! 2 Timothy 1:7 says, *"For God did not give us a spirit of fear but of power and love and **self-control.***" (NET Bible) Galatians 5:23 says, *"The fruit of the Spirit includes SELF-CONTROL, and the Spirit is in you!"*

4. **Believe YOU are in control.** As you control your thoughts, you will control your emotions. THEN, you will not feel the urge to control others!

5. **You CAN remember what happiness is.** Jeremiah FORGOT what happiness was because he talked himself into misery. When he began to think about the goodness of God, JOY WAS RESTORED. Emotions follow thoughts—whether good or bad.

6. **Express your emotions UPWARD, and you won't need to always express them OUTWARD.** When you pour your heart and feelings out to God (no matter how bad they may be), the temptation to explode at others will be diminished.

THINK IT AND SAY IT

I am not under the control of my emotions anymore. They are under my control. As I fill my mind with good thoughts, they will become good emotions. I can control my emotions through my thought life, and my thought life is surrendered to God's Word. I have self-control over my life because of the Spirit within me. And from this day forward, my emotions serve me, rather than control me. I will pour my emotions out to God, and I don't need to pour them out to others, in Jesus' Name!

Scriptures

- Proverbs 23:7
- Proverbs 16:31–32
- Psalm 13:1–6

Day 25

"God Must Be Rewarding Them and Not Me."

Today we're fasting from the thought that says: **"God must be rewarding them and not me."** One of the things that makes us most unhappy is when we compare ourselves to others and to what they have. When we compare, we despair. So . . .

LET'S CHANGE IT TODAY

1. **God has enough for EVERYONE.** Psalm 145:16 says that He satisfies the desire of EVERY living thing. His reward for one person doesn't come at the expense of someone else.

2. **What do you desire?** Freedom? Joy? Provision? A better relationship with someone? He will satisfy your desire. Ask Him to right now.

3. **SETTLE THIS: God honors His Word above anything.** Cling to His Word, and you will get honored with it. **Promotion, increase, and rewards will come.**

4. **Get your thoughts off THEM and on HIM.** Fix your eyes on Jesus. He is the source of all that you could

ever want or need. Every good and perfect gift comes from above (James 1:17). Look UP, not OUT.

5. **It's easier to seek Him than you think.** Seeking God is not about our effort. It's about LOOKING TO Jesus as your source and discovering His way of thinking and seeing things. As we think His way (His Word), we will believe like Him. Our faith will soar! Manifestations WILL COME. That is what it means to seek Him.

6. **See other people's promotions or rewards as a PREDICTION of yours.** The testimony of what Jesus has done for someone else is a prophecy of what He can do for you.

7. **Expect favor.** Favor surrounds the righteous on every side! And you are the righteousness of God, simply by being in Christ.

THINK IT AND SAY IT

God is MY Rewarder. I adopt His thinking regarding my life and situation. I fix my eyes on Him, and He finishes my faith. Favor surrounds me, abundance surrounds me, and God's rewards surround me like a shield, in Jesus' Name!

Scriptures

- Psalm 145:16
- Psalm 138:2
- Hebrews 12:2
- James 1:17
- Hebrews 11:6
- Revelation 19:10
- Psalm 5:12

"I Feel Stuck."

Today we are fasting from the thought that says, **"I feel stuck."**

We've all thought that at times, but it's a lie. There's always a way out of what you're in, or a way into what you've been kept out of.

The devil would love for you to believe you are stuck, and that there's no way out of the situation you're experiencing. He wants you discouraged, immobilized, and paralyzed.

LET'S CHANGE IT TODAY

1. **Believe in the ministry of the Holy Spirit today.** Romans 8:26 says, *"We don't always know how to pray as we should, but the Spirit intercedes for us."* No matter what your situation is, the Holy Spirit knows how to bring about God's will for your life, as you ask and thank Him.

2. **Think this thought today: PRAYER CHANGES THINGS.** There's nothing you can't impact through prayer. Prayer gets you unstuck. It gets you moving again. Prayer is powerful. *"And all things, whatsoever you shall **ask** in prayer, believing, **you shall receive"*** (Matthew 21:22).

3. **Believe that faith finds a way. Whenever I feel stuck, I remember these words: FAITH FINDS A WAY.** In Mark 2:1–5, the friends of the paralyzed man could not find a way into the house where Jesus was. They were stuck, but *they believed there was another way.* They went up on the roof and lowered him down through the ceiling tiles, and the man was healed. Why? Because faith found a way! If we don't think it, we won't look for it.

4. **Remember, Jesus is the 4th man in the fire.** When it seemed like the three men in Daniel 3 were going to be burned in the fiery furnace, Jesus showed up! What was an impossible situation was made possible, because Jesus was with them. And He is with you now!

5. **Jesus is your way.** *"I am the way, the truth, and the life." **He is the way** when there just seems to be no way. **He is your way** out of whatever situation you are in. Expect Him to make a way.

6. **Just think next step.** When Jesus was tempted to not go to the cross, the Bible says, *"He went forward a little . . ."* (Mark 14:35, KJV). When you feel stuck, like there's nothing you can do, just take a step. Don't think about all the steps. Just take the next one. In a relationship, the first step may be just saying you're

sorry. If it's finances, maybe it's just cutting one area of spending or giving one extra offering. Move forward a little!

THINK IT AND SAY IT

The Holy Spirit is interceding for me when I feel stuck. He is moving in me and through me. **I think and believe there is always a way.** Even when it seems like there is no way, Jesus is the Way. He is with me no matter what fire I'm facing. When I feel stuck, I will think about one step I can take that will move me towards healing, blessing, and God's will for my life, in Jesus' Name!

Scriptures

- Romans 8:26

- Matthew 21:22

- Mark 2:1–5

Day 27

"I Feel Alone."

In Mark 4, when the disciples tried to cross over to the other side of the sea in the boat, they were overwhelmed by the storm that struck their ship. They feared for their lives, bailing out water furiously. Have you ever been in a storm? The waters crash against you. You feel helpless. You feel alone. You cry out, *"Lord, where are you? Don't you care?"*

The disciples forgot one small detail in the midst of their storm: Jesus was in the boat with them. There was nothing greater than His presence!

Let's overcome the thought that says, *"**I feel alone.** Where is God when I need Him most?"*

LET'S CHANGE IT TODAY

1. **He is in the boat with you!** In Mark 4:36–40, Jesus was asleep in the boat. Someone asked me once, "How do we wake Jesus up, when He is asleep in our boat, in the middle of a storm?" Well, I said, "You don't wake Him up. You rest with Him!" If He's not worried, don't you worry. HIS PRESENCE calmed the storm then, just as it will do now.

2. **The disciples didn't need Jesus to awake.** They needed to awake to the fact that God was with them.

When you know He is with you, there is nothing to fear. Psalm 23:4 says, *"Though I walk through the valley of the shadow of death, I will fear NO EVIL, for You are with me!"*

3. **Great miracle = Jesus calmed the storm. Greater miracle = Jesus slept IN THE MIDST of the storm.** When you realize He is in your boat with you, you will have supernatural peace. Calming the storm is great; peace in the midst of it is greater!

4. **DO NOT MISTAKE FIRE IN YOUR LIFE FOR GOD'S ABSENCE.** In Daniel 3:22–25, Jesus was the fourth man in the fire with Shadrach, Meshach, and Abednego. He was present in the middle of the fire. Just because you don't feel His presence, doesn't mean He isn't there. BELIEVE HE IS WITH YOU, and eventually your situation will FEEL HIS PRESENCE!

5. **Psalm 91:10 says, *"No evil shall befall you, nor shall any plague come near your tent."*** The next verse says, "For He will give His angel(s) charge concerning you." There are many angels involved in our lives, but this is talking about HIS ANGEL. The Old Testament "Angel" is Jesus Christ himself. He is Lord; therefore He has charge concerning us!

THINK IT AND SAY IT

I am not trying to get in God's presence; I am already in, through the blood of Jesus. He is in my boat with me. He is not "over there." He is "here" right now—with me and in me!

I awake to the fact that He is with me. There is no separation. I can rest with Him, in the midst of any storm. I can walk with Him in the midst of the fire.

I am fearless because He is with me. Therefore, no evil shall befall me, nor shall any plague come near my dwelling place—my church, my home, my body, or my life—in Jesus' Name!

Scriptures

- Psalm 23:4

- Psalm 91:9–16

Day 28

"This Is a Scary Time to be Living In."

Today we're fasting from the thought that says, **"This is a scary time to be living in."**

When you look around at all the news and evil in the world— whether it's natural disasters, terror, rumors of wars, disease, depression, etc., it can be pretty scary.

There is much fear in this world, but it doesn't have to control you or your loved ones!

LET'S CHANGE IT TODAY

1. **Know your authority.** In Luke 10:19, Jesus said: *"Behold I have given you authority . . . over all the power of the enemy."* The devil doesn't push us around. We push him around! Whatever we bind on earth is bound in heaven—Matthew 18:18. You're never afraid of what you have authority over.

2. **Receive peace as a gift!** Simply accept it today! Jesus said: *My peace I GIVE you, not as the world gives*—John 14:27. We receive peace, not as something dependent on circumstances—it is a gift. Therefore, we don't have to be afraid.

3. **Remember what you have—and what you "have not."** 2 Timothy 1:7 says, *"God has NOT given you a spirit of fear; but POWER, LOVE, and a SOUND MIND."*

4. **Take your daily "pre-Scripture" as your new "prescription."** Take a dose of Psalm 91:10, which declares, *"NO evil or harm shall befall you, nor shall any disaster or plague come near your tent!"*

5. **Meditate on good news from Job.** Job 5:19 says, *"He will deliver you from six troubles; in seven no evil shall touch you."* Seven is the number of perfection. Through the blood of Jesus, He will perfectly protect you!

6 **Love conquers all.** As you fill your mind with God's love towards you, FEAR LEAVES under any circumstance.

7. **In the darkest of times, God presents His most stunning performances.** Expect God to show up!

THINK IT AND SAY IT

I receive the gift of PEACE, and therefore I am not troubled. I have power, love, and a sound mind. I have authority over the enemy. No evil or disaster can harm me. God is my Deliverer. I expect God to show up in my life today, in Jesus' name.

Scriptures

- Luke 10:19
- John 14:27
- 2 Timothy 1:7
- Job 5:19
- 1 John 4:18–19
- 1 John 3:1
- 2 Corinthians 4:6

Day 29

"I Feel Stressed Out."

Today we are fasting from the thought that says, **"I feel stressed out."**

Stress is a powerful mindset that we are going to dismantle. It is a collection of thoughts or fears that bear down on your mind until they penetrate you and control your emotions, your health, and your relationships.

LET'S CHANGE IT TODAY

1. **Know your enemy.** The real enemy is *thinking* that you have to get rid of the enemy. Psalm 23:5 says that He prepares a table (celebration) *in the presence of your enemies.* Begin to celebrate and praise God in the midst of the pressure, problem, or bad news. That's when the enemy loses its power.

2. **The Prince of Peace lives in you!** (Colossians 1:27) Peace comes from the presence of God, not the absence of problems. Meditate on the fact that God's presence is in you and with you. Jesus said *"I am with you always."*

3. **Your treasure is greater than your trouble.** In 2 Corinthians 4:6–8, Paul said, *"We are troubled on every side, but not stressed."* Why? Because he knew

he had a treasure inside, the power to speak God's Word, and the ability change the situation.

4. **Be certain you are going to make it.** Uncertainty is a source of stress. Jesus had peace and, in Mark 4, He even slept in the midst of a violent storm. How? Because He declared, *"We are going to the other side."* God's words create certainty and certainty eliminates stress!

5. **You're not *under* stress; you're *over* it!** You are seated with Christ in heavenly places—Ephesians 2:1–6. Live life from above—from God's perspective. You're above ONLY and not underneath (Deuteronomy 28:13). The battle is already won. Jesus did it all. Your fight is simply to believe that. That's when stress leaves.

THINK IT AND SAY IT

I am free from the power of stress. I don't have to get rid of all my problems to get rid of stress. I have a table in the presence of my enemies. They have NO power over me.

The Prince of Peace lives in me. I am certain I will make it. I am going to the other side. The battle is already won. Jesus did it all. My treasure is greater than my trouble, and I am above stress and not underneath it, in Jesus' Name!

Scriptures

- Psalm 23:5
- Colossians 1:27
- Matthew 28:20
- 2 Corinthians 4:6–8
- Ephesians 2:1–6
- Deuteronomy 28:13

Day 30

"What's Wrong With Me?"

Our Fast From Wrong Thinking is working! Stay on
this journey with me. These seeds will produce the great
harvests you have always wanted and needed in every area
of your life.

Today we're fasting from the thought that says, **"What's
wrong with me?"**

The constant awareness of our "falling short" is where the
devil and religion wants to keep us. This keeps us defeated
and hemmed in by shame, rather than liberated through
our divine nature. 2 Peter 1:4 says, "Through His promises, we share in the divine nature of God and escape the
corruption that is in the world through lust."

LET'S CHANGE IT TODAY

1. **Understand the gift of righteousness.** 2 Corinthians 5:21 says, *"He who knew NO sin, was made to be
   sin FOR US, that we would be MADE the righteousness
   of God."* This is the greatest EXCHANGE in human
   history! Jesus took our sinfulness and imparted to us
   His righteousness—which means we are RIGHT in
   God's eyes, not wrong.

2. **Awake to righteousness.** 1 Corinthians 15:34 (AMP) says, *"Awaken to righteousness; and you will not sin."* When God thinks of you, He thinks of a victorious, conquering, strong, powerful, wise, and holy son or daughter. He sees you as a mighty champion—the head and not the tail. Righteousness means: to stand in His presence without a sense of guilt, shame, inferiority, or condemnation.

3. **Reject sin-consciousness.** When you are always conscious of what's wrong, you will DO wrong. When you are always conscious of BEING the righteousness of God—you will DO right. You'll act on the outside how you see yourself on the inside.

4. **Ask the Holy Spirit to do what He does best.** 1 Corinthians 2:12 says, *". . . We have received the Spirit of God, so that we may know the things freely given to us by God."* A key ministry of the Holy Spirit is to REVEAL what is already yours (NOT TO REVEAL TO YOU ALL THAT IS WRONG IN YOUR LIFE).

5. **Dwell on what's right rather than what's wrong.** Go through the Scripture regarding who you are in Christ, what is yours in Christ, and what you can do in Christ. It's staggering. Flood your mind with this new way of thinking.

THINK IT AND SAY IT

I am the righteousness of God, through the blood of Jesus. I stand in the presence of God without guilt, shame, inferiority, or condemnation. I awake to righteousness and believe it will lead me to a victorious life. I am a joint heir with Jesus. When God looks at me, He sees His blood. He thinks of me as a conquering, powerful, and holy son or daughter. I will not think of myself as anything less or more than what God thinks of me in Jesus' Name!

Scriptures

- 2 Peter 1:4

- 1 Corinthians 15:34

- Deuteronomy 28:13

Day 31

"I Feel Angry."

Today, we are fasting from anger—thoughts like, **"I feel angry,"** or, **"They make me so mad."**

Anger is a powerful emotion that obviously can hurt ourselves and others. It leads to bad decisions, damaged relationships, stress, and physical sickness.

LET'S CHANGE IT TODAY

1. **Discover the power within you.** Remember, anger comes from a sense of powerlessness. When we feel powerless to change something, we get afraid, leading us to anger. 2 Timothy 1:7 says, *"God has not given us a spirit of fear, but power, love, and a sound mind."* Meditate on this verse. You have power.

2. **Listen quickly and speak slowly.** James 1:19 says, *"Be quick to hear, slow to speak, then the result is that you will be slow to anger!"* Follow this simple pattern, and anger will lose its grip.

3. **Realize that anger does not work.** It doesn't produce or *achieve* anything. James 1:20 says, *"For the anger of man does not achieve (work, produce) the righteousness of God."* If you had an employee that didn't work, produce, or achieve, you would fire them, right? *Fire* your anger from your life. It doesn't achieve anything.

4. **Deal with unresolved conflict *today!*** Ephesians 4:26 says, *"Do not let the sun go down on your anger."* Make peace with whomever you have something against today. Don't let it fester. You'll be amazed at how much less you will feel angry.

5. **It's OK to feel anger, but direct it the right way—towards the devil.** Notice, the next verse goes on to say, "Don't give the devil an opportunity to work" (Ephesians 4:27). The devil wants you to blame others for your anger. But realize, there's no one to blame but the devil! And like a soldier with a machine gun, who just discovered the enemy, turn your weapons completely on him. Use your anger to resist the devil by speaking the Word with an aggressive force, and eliminate his opportunity to work!

6. **Get the whole picture.** So often, the reason we get mad or afraid is that we only see a snapshot of what's really going on. As soon as anger comes, ask God to open your eyes to see the big picture. He did it for Elisha's servant. He will do it for you!

THINK IT AND SAY IT

I am free from the power of anger. I have power over it! I have power, love, and a sound mind. I will not act rashly, but choose to listen quickly and speak slowly. I say to anger: **You are fired!**

I refuse to blame anyone for my angry feelings. I will use my aggressive feelings against the devil by speaking the Word of God and resisting him <u>firmly</u> in my faith today, in Jesus' Name!

Scriptures

- 2 Timothy 1:7
- James 1:19–20
- Ephesians 4:17,26
- 2 Kings 6:16–17

Day 32

"How Could I Ever Recover from This Loss?"

We've all lost something at one time or another. If it hasn't been money, it's been time, relationships, opportunity, peace, or HOPE. Well, today we begin to GET IT BACK!

Today we're fasting from the thought that says, **"How could I ever recover from this loss?"**

LET'S CHANGE IT TODAY

1. **Let this thought permeate your mind: God is a God of restoration.** Joel 2:25–26 says, *"I will restore the years that have been lost."* Whether it's lost years, lost opportunity, lost finances, bad decisions, or what others have done to you—God will restore. **He is the God of restoration.**

2. **Ditch the mentality of *settling*.** We must refuse to settle. The ten lepers wouldn't settle for their leprosy. They cried out to Jesus. The woman with the demon-possessed daughter wouldn't settle with her daughter's condition (Matthew 15:22). Bartimaeus wouldn't settle with blindness. He wouldn't stop until he recovered his sight. REFUSE to settle for the way things are.

3. **Realize that God WANTS you to go to Him and to ask Him to avenge you.** In Luke 18, the unjust judge avenged the widow because of her persistence. HOW MUCH MORE will our just and loving God avenge His children!

4. **All the promises of God are YES.** He has promised restoration and recovery—so ask Him for them TODAY. God wants you to recover more than you do. Believe this.

5. **Believe the promise: the thief has to repay sevenfold what he's stolen.** The devil is the thief. And Jesus has defeated him. He has given us authority over him. You have the right to get your stuff back. Jesus paid for it. Whatever good thing that has been lost in your life, is coming back.

6. **Prophesy to the dry bones in your life.** Speak to whatever is lost and command it to come back. Use your words. Job 22:28 says, *"I shall decree a thing and it will be so."*

7. **Expect recovery!** *"You shall surely overtake your enemies and you shall recover all"* (1 Samuel 30:8). Restoration and the recovery of what has been lost in our lives is a divine promise. Stand on it today.

THINK IT AND SAY IT

I will recover all that has been lost in my life. I expect the restoration of lost relationships, lost money, lost hope, and lost opportunities. I will not settle for loss and lack. God will avenge me. He will restore what has been stolen from me. I ask Him and expect Him to avenge me of all that has been lost in my life. I call forth a sevenfold return of what has been taken from me, in Jesus' Name!

Scriptures

- Joel 2:25–26

- Luke 18:6–7

- 2 Corinthians 1:20

- Ezekiel 37:4–8

Day 33

"God Is Mad At Me."

Today we are fasting from the thought that says, **"God is mad at me."**

Many people think the reason bad things are happening is because God is mad or against them. Or perhaps you don't think He's overtly against you, but that He's just not aggressively helping you. If you think God is mad at you, you'll feel discouraged and rejected. You won't expect good things to happen.

Let's take this thought captive. The word, *captive*, means: "to conquer with a sword." We conquer wrong thinking with the sword of God's Word!

LET'S CHANGE IT TODAY

1. **God is not mad at you; He is mad about you!** This is something I started saying many years ago when I discovered God's love. When you accept this thought, you will have confidence, expectation, and peace. How do I know this is true? Romans 8:38–39 says, *"Nothing can separate you from the love of God . . ."* You are forgiven, and you are LOVED.

2. **Think this new thought: God loves me as much as He loves Jesus.** In John 17:23, Jesus says to the

Father, ". . . that the world may know that You sent Me, *and loved them, as much as You have loved Me.*" What an amazing truth. God loves you as much as He loves Jesus!

3. **He thinks precious thoughts about you all the time!** Psalm 139:17–18 says, *"How precious are Your thoughts toward me, O God . . . If I should count them, they would outnumber the sand. When I awake, I am still with You!"*

4. **What God said to Jesus is the same for you.** *"You are My beloved Son. In You, I am well-pleased."* (Mark 1:11) Hallelujah! He doesn't sound mad at Jesus. He sounds mad about Him! Well, 1 John 4:17 says, *"As He is, so are we."*

5. **There is nothing God is holding back from you.** Romans 8:32 says, *"He who did not spare His own Son, but delivered Him up for us all, how shall He not also with Him freely give us all things."* Rejoice in this truth!

6. **You are not condemned.** Romans 8:1 says, *"There is no condemnation for those who are in Christ Jesus . . ."* God approves of you because of your faith in Jesus, not because you have done everything right. God's love for you is non-negotiable. Jeremiah 31:3 says He loves you with an everlasting love. It is an unstoppable love!

God is not mad at me; He is mad about me. He loves me as much as Jesus. He thinks precious thoughts about me all the time. I am His beloved, and He is mine!

There is nothing God is holding back from me. He didn't hold back His best; therefore He won't hold back the rest.

I refuse to be condemned. I am forgiven. I reject the thought that He is mad at me or against me. God is for me and not against me. His love toward me is unstoppable, in Jesus' Name!

Scriptures

- Romans 8:38–39
- Ephesians 1:7
- 1 John 4:10
- John 17:23
- Psalm 139:17–18

"Things Aren't Getting Better, They Are Getting Worse!"

Today we're fasting from the thought that says, **"Things aren't getting better, they are getting worse!"**

This thinking is not an option today or EVER! No matter how bad things have gotten financially or in ANY AREA OF YOUR LIFE, God has promised that they will get better.

LET'S CHANGE IT TODAY

1. **The path of the righteous gets brighter and brighter until the full day.** Expect it to get brighter today!

2. **You have a covenant of increase from God.** Psalm 115:14 says, *"May the Lord give you increase."* Deuteronomy 1:11 says, *"May the Lord increase you a thousand times and bless you as He has promised."* Expect!

3. **Eliminate the "half empty glass" mentality.** In fact, don't accept it "half full" either! Think: My cup runs over!

4. **Your life is going to end up better than it started!** Ecclesiastes 7:8 says, *"Better is the end of a thing than the beginning."* Haggai 2:9 says, *"The latter days of this house shall be greater than the former."*

5. **Look at how God does things.** He takes us from law to grace; from sin to righteousness; from sickness to health; from defeat to victory; therefore, expect things to get better and better in every area of your life.

6. **EXPECT THE BEST TODAY!** In Luke 15:22 the father said, *"bring the best robe, and put it on my son"* You are God's child. He wants the best for you. Believe for goodness and mercy to follow you all the days of your life.

THINK IT AND SAY IT

No matter what is happening in this world, things are getting better and better for me! God has made me righteous through His blood; therefore, my path is getting brighter and brighter every day.

My inner man is being renewed, day by day. I have a covenant of increase and God is increasing me, and all that I have, more and more. I expect the best today. He has saved the best for last, and therefore I expect my coming days to be better than my past days, in Jesus' Name!

Scriptures

- Proverbs 4:18
- Psalm 115:14
- Deuteronomy 1:11
- Haggai 2:9

"I'm Overwhelmed."

Today we are fasting from the feelings and thoughts that say, **"I'm overwhelmed!"**

Everything you see in this world was created by God in six days. He's in the business of getting a lot accomplished in little time. And He lives in you! You don't have to carry your burden alone. Most people don't understand what Jesus meant when He said, "Take My yoke upon you."

A yoke is a harness placed upon two oxen. It causes them to plow together. So, when one gets weak or overwhelmed, he can continue by being pulled by the other. When we feel weighed down, we need to remember, we are yoked to Him. Jesus is attached to us and will carry the load for us.

LET'S CHANGE IT TODAY

1. **Cast your cares upon God.** He will care for you. How? Be honest. Tell Him what's wrong. Ask Him to carry it for you and believe He will. Remember, after you give Him your cares, don't run to pick them back up. Trust Jesus to carry the load for you.

2. **See yourself attached, or yoked, to God.** He holds you up and pulls you up when you are weak

and overwhelmed. You are one with Him. When you feel weak and burdened, remember that He is carrying you.

3. **Begin to believe that you can handle anything.** Start believing this today. Mark 9:23 says, *"All things are possible for those who believe."*

4. **Feast on this thought: nothing is too difficult for God.** If nothing is too difficult for Him, and He lives in you, then nothing is too difficult for you. You will make it!

5. **God will complete those things that concern you.** As you surrender those concerns to God, they become His responsibility. He will complete, fulfill, perfect, and bring those things to pass. He will lift your burden and finish what He started in your life.

THINK IT AND SAY IT

I can handle anything today because I am yoked to Jesus. Today I refuse to be overwhelmed. I cast all my cares on Jesus. He cares for me and will carry my load.

Nothing is too difficult for God. Therefore, I declare that nothing is too difficult for me today! He is the author and finisher of my faith, in Jesus' Name!

Scriptures

- Matthew 11:29–30
- 1 Peter 5:7
- Mark 9:23
- Jeremiah 32:17
- Psalm 138:8

A Negative Attitude

Today we're fasting from **a negative attitude.**

Attitude IS everything. It is a mindset that takes precedence over all other facts. And I want us to obliterate negativity from our lives. You CAN control whether life is easy or hard, by your attitude. So many people look at things in a negative way, expect negative things to happen, and speak themselves into negative results. They never grow. So . . .

LET'S CHANGE IT TODAY

1. **God is a YES God.** 2 Corinthians 1:20—*"All the promises of God are YES!"* He says YES to everything He has promised. He's a positive God. And you are made in His image.

2. **CAN IT!** Success comes in CANS, not in cannots! Philippians 4:13 says, *"I CAN do all things through Christ which strengthens me."*

3. **Get rid of the NEGATIVE PSYCHIC in you.** The "negative psychic" in you presumes you know what people are thinking about you and it's usually bad. "She thinks I'm an idiot"; "I can tell he's always judging me" . . . etc. The only person's thoughts

that matter about you are God's and THEY ARE GOOD.

4. **Stop seeing giants around you. And start seeing the giant in you!** Greater is He that is in you. Begin to see yourself conquering everything!

5. **Be a thermostat, not a thermometer.** A thermostat SETS the temperature. It doesn't read it. **Set the thermostat of your attitude to "ABOVE ONLY" thinking.** Deuteronomy 28:13 says, *"You will be ABOVE ONLY and not beneath."* The NIV says, *"YOU WILL ALWAYS BE AT THE TOP."* Refuse to accept any other way of thinking or living.

6. **Make your greatest discovery today!** The greatest discovery in life is that you can change your life by changing the attitude of your mind. Jesus said, *"If you can believe, all things are possible."*

THINK IT AND SAY IT

My life is getting easier not harder! I focus on the good things God has done in my life. I believe all things are possible! I expect opportunity, promotion, and success to come my way because I am a believer. I'm above ONLY and not beneath. I am the head and not the tail. My attitude of faith and expectation takes precedence over all other facts . . . beginning today, in Jesus' Name!

Scriptures

- 2 Corinthians 1:20
- Psalm 139:17–18
- Numbers 13:30
- Romans 8:37
- Mark 9:23
- Deuteronomy 28:13

"I Feel Guilty."

Today we are fasting from the thought that says, **"I feel guilty."**

We've all had thoughts that try to make us feel guilty, such as: "You don't do enough. Look at what you've done wrong. You're not good enough. You don't say the right things. You don't measure up. You don't do as much for others as you should. You eat too much."

This line of thinking produces guilt, which leads to self-hatred, anger toward others, bad decisions, harsh words, procrastination, and fear.

LET'S CHANGE IT TODAY

1. **Jesus declares you:** *not guilty.* This doesn't mean that you've never sinned or done wrong. This means that He washed away all your sin and guilt with His blood. The Word of God declares Jesus as our guilt offering, thus declaring us free from guilt.

2. **See what God sees.** Accept Colossians 1:22, which says that through Jesus' blood, *"He presents you holy and faultless and unblamable in the Father's eyes."* When God sees you, He sees Jesus—like when Jacob went before his father Isaac with the hair, skin, and

scent of his brother. The father saw Jacob as if he were Esau. And He sees you as if you were Jesus—without guilt.

3. **Meditate on Job 10:7.** *"According to your knowledge, I am indeed not guilty . . ."* (NASB) When a person is born again, they are cleansed of sin and guilt by the blood of Jesus, and therefore *not guilty.*

4. **When you blow it, don't deny it.** Admit it. Confess it. 1 John 1:9 says, *"If you confess your sin, He is faithful and just to forgive you and to **cleanse you from all unrighteousness."***

5. **It's already done! Believe that it is already done.** The last words of Jesus on the cross were, *"It is finished."* At that moment, the price was paid for your sin and guilt. Hebrews 1:3 says, *"He cleansed us from our sin."*

6. **Stop thinking that you have to feel guilty to be forgiven.** Sometimes we think we owe it to people to feel guilty and bad for everything. Stop thinking that. You don't owe anyone anything. Don't think guilt somehow pays for something. The blood of Jesus paid it all. When we feel like we owe God guilt or we owe it to others to wallow in guilt, it's an insult to His blood.

7. Stop beating yourself up about what you haven't done. We often punish ourselves with self-condemnation. We will *never* do enough for God. That's why Jesus did it all. He *paid* for sin, the curse, and our failure. *Our job is to believe.*

THINK IT AND SAY IT

Jesus has declared me **not guilty.** Even when I feel I don't do enough, or that I'm not good enough, God says that **faith in Him is enough.**

I don't have to feel guilty to be forgiven. I am forgiven by faith in Jesus.

Today I stop beating myself up about all that I've done or haven't done.

I don't have to be perfect. He already is—therefore, I rest my faith in Him, in Jesus' Name!

Scriptures

- Hebrews 7:27

- Colossians 1:22

- Job 10:7

- Hebrews 1:3

Day 38

"Why Isn't God Stopping This?"

Today we're fasting from the thought that says, **"Why isn't God stopping this?"**

This thinking is rooted in the inaccurate belief that God is in control of everything. Don't get me wrong: He started this world in control of everything, but He gave much authority to mankind at Creation; and then again as new creations, in Christ. We have to stop waiting for God to stop the things He gave us the power to stop. Jesus said: *Whatever we bind on earth is bound in heaven.*

LET'S CHANGE IT TODAY

1. **You have authority in life.** Remember, Jesus has given us ALL power over the enemy (Luke 10:19). The enemy, the devil, wants to blind you to your authority, so that you will accept whatever happens in life, or wait for God to do something about it. Awaken to your God-given authority as a child of God.

2. **Start reigning and you'll stop whining.** *"Through the abundance of grace and the gift of righteousness, we REIGN in life."* (Romans 5:17) As you awake to grace and righteousness—and your God-given authority— **you'll stop thinking and feeling like a victim.**

3. **God gives every GOOD gift.** (James 1:17) God is good, and the devil is bad. It was Satan, not God, who smote Job. But God has given us the power to resist the devil, and walk in our God-given authority and destiny.

4. **God doesn't send storms to teach us a lesson.** Life brings storms. But God brings shelter. God is the source of our *shelter*, not the source of the *storm*. Isaiah 25:4 says, "You are a refuge from the storm."

5. **Plant the right seeds BEFORE the storms of life hit.** (Mark 4:26–35) Jesus taught His disciples to plant the seed of God's Word. THEN, He got in the boat, and the storm hit. They had the power to stop the storm. They just didn't know it.

6. **You're just like Jesus!** Yes, the disciples woke Jesus, and He stopped the storm. BUT, in 1 John 4:17, it tells us that as He is, so are we. He gave you His Word and His authority. You can stop the forces of hell that come against you.

7. **Wisdom is greater than the storm.** And the wise build their house—their life—on the Word of God. No matter what life or the enemy throws at you, you will stand—especially when your life is built on the wisdom of God's Word.

THINK IT AND SAY IT

I agree with Jesus! I take authority over the storms of life, and over all the power of the enemy. Through the abundance of grace and the gift of righteousness, I reign in life. I have the power to choose PEACE in the midst of the storms of life. I walk in wisdom, by acting on the Word, and I rise above every situation, in the Name of Jesus!

Scriptures

- Luke 10:19

- Romans 5:17

- Job 2:7

- James 1:17

- 1 John 4:17

- Matthew 7:24–25

"It's Too Late."

We are so time conscious. We allow time to limit us and define for us what we're capable of, or what God can do in our lives.

Today we're fasting from the thought that says, **"It's too late."**

It's often ingrained in us that it's too late to change, too late to start a new career, too late to save your marriage, too late to recover from a terrible mistake, too late to start over again, or too late to have a second chance.

The truth is: It's never too late!

When you realize that it's not too late, you have hope. You take action. You move forward.

LET'S CHANGE IT TODAY

1. **UN-DECIDE that it's too late for these things to change.** *Un-decide* that you can't recover. *Un-decide* that the damage is irreversible. It's NOT too late to turn your finances around, to recover from a tragedy or mistake, to surrender your life to God, to take better care of yourself, to change the way you see yourself, to apologize, or to break a bad habit.

2. **Meditate on the fact that God created time and He can multiply it.** The earth and sun stood still in Joshua 10:12–13. *"And Joshua said in the sight of Israel, 'Sun, stand still.' So the sun stood still, and the moon stopped."* Joshua had control over time for God's purpose. We need to start thinking that way—that we have control over our time, rather than it having control over us!

3. **Think about the great cloud of witnesses for whom it wasn't too late.**

   - It wasn't too late for Abraham and Sarah to become parents at 99 and 90 years old.

   - It wasn't too late for Peter after he denied the Lord three times.

   - It wasn't too late for the woman caught in adultery (John 8:1–11), the woman with the issue of blood (Mark 5:25–34), or the man who was lame at the pool of Bethesda for 38 years (John 5:1–10).

4. **Embrace grace.** Lamentations 3:22–23 says, "His mercy is new every morning." Hebrews 4:15 says, *"Come boldly to the throne of grace to receive mercy and grace in your time of need."* **Mercy** is when God doesn't give us the judgment that we do deserve, and **grace** is when God gives us the goodness that we don't deserve.

5. **Rid yourself of excuse-making.** God doesn't accept excuses, but He gives lots of grace! We might feel low self-esteem or have a disability as Moses did. He had a speech impediment, but God gave him chance after chance to be used to deliver God's people.

6. **Ask God for more time and another chance.** Hezekiah did this in 2 Kings 20:1–6. When Hezekiah asked for a second chance, God told him, *"I have heard your prayer . . . surely I will heal you . . . and I will add to your days fifteen years."* If he did it for Hezekiah, He will do it for you!

THINK IT & SAY IT

It's not too late for things to improve in my life and radically turn around. I believe in the God of second chances. I can recover, and there is nothing that God won't turn around in my life. God created time, and He can multiply it for me. I am not controlled by time. By God's grace, I control it, in Jesus' Name!

Scriptures

- Joshua 10:12–13

- Lamentations 3:22–23

- Hebrews 4:15

"I'm Limited."

Today we're fasting from the thought that says, **"I'm limited."**

Perhaps you've felt limited by your past, your upbringing, or your pain. We all have something we think may limit us.

LET'S CHANGE IT TODAY

1. **God is able!** He will do above and beyond all you can ask or think. (Ephesians 3:20) He's not limited, and so neither are you, because you are made in His image.

2. **Meet Jephthah!** His past told him that he was the son of a prostitute. But God told him he was a mighty warrior! Each one of us has conflicting voices telling us who we are. You must choose God's version of yourself, rather than people's version of you. Side with what God says about you.

3. **Leave the room.** The father of faith, Abraham, felt confined and limited by his inability to have a child with his wife Sarah. So God brought Abraham out of the house, and told him to look UP and count the stars. Whenever you feel limited, walk outside and look up. Look to God.

4. **You can only see stars when you're looking up!** Repeat step 3 above! Stop looking at the ceiling and start looking at the stars.

5. **Get in touch with your new spirit.** Your spirit is your vertical window, giving you the ability to look up and see from God's point of view. Your flesh is your horizontal window, allowing you only to look around at your circumstance or to look back at your past limitations. Open your vertical window and look up, expecting God to do above and beyond all you can ask or think!

6. **Living beyond your wildest expectations and dreams starts with some wild expectations and dreams!** Dream big. Ask big. Expect big! He will do infinitely above and beyond your highest thoughts and dreams!

7. **Don't limit God.** Psalm 78:41 says, *"They limited the Holy One of Israel."* (KJV) We limit Him when we think small, dream small, and ask small. Jabez prayed: ENLARGE MY TERRITORY. (1 Chronicles 4:9–10) Ask that today.

I side with what God says about me today. I am a mighty warrior. I will not be defined or confined by my past. I refuse to be limited by my failure, mistakes, or the limitations others have put on me.

I leave the room where the ceiling is, and I look up. I look up, expecting God to do exceedingly abundantly above and beyond my highest hopes, thoughts, desires, and dreams!

Today I ask God to bless me indeed and enlarge my territory; I refuse to limit Him, and therefore I will break through, in Jesus' Name!

Scriptures

- Ephesians 3:20

- Judges 11:1

- Genesis 15:5

- 1 Chronicles 4:9–10

Conclusion

Now that you've begun this revolution, *From the Inside Out*, let me encourage you with a few final thoughts:

1. **Expect things to get better!** Don't be discouraged if the miracle you need doesn't happen overnight. Fasting from wrong thinking is a process. It's the cocoon that awakens the power and beautiful destiny within you!

2. **Review regularly.** The devil will try to pull you back into wrong thinking. Whenever a negative thought comes back, speak to it with the thoughts and words in this book.

3. **Share your story!** Something that will keep you walking in victory is sharing how God has changed your life! Please send me your testimony at www.gregorydickow.com. It will inspire someone else to experience the freedom and change they've been longing for!

4. **Be a part of changing the world!** This is a movement born of God that changes people from the inside out! You can help bring this revolution to millions of others around the world by sowing a seed of any amount. Just log onto www.fastfromwrongthinking.com and click on *"Sow A Seed."* Stand with me in getting the

word out about this life-changing Fast From Wrong Thinking. Remember, "As a man thinks within, so is he!" (Proverbs 23:7)

5. **Finally, don't ever forget this powerful truth: There is no stopping the man or woman who is set free from wrong thinking!**

Other Books
by Gregory Dickow

- **The Power to Change Today**

- **Breaking the Power of Inferiority**

- **Conquering Your Flesh**

- **Taking Charge of Your Emotions**

- **Silencing the Accuser**

- **Changed by Love**

- **30 Pearls of Pure Grace**

- **How to Fulfill God's Purpose for Your Life**

You can order these and many other life-changing materials by calling toll-free **1-888-849-5433** or visiting **www.gregorydickow.com.**

Also, prayerfully consider becoming a **Love Revolution Partner** with Pastor Gregory Dickow . . . changing the world one life at a time!

For more information about Gregory Dickow Ministries please visit **www.gregorydickow.com.**